The Mind Diet:
Detox

F.J. Roberts & J.D. Roberts

The Mind Diet: Detox

CONTENTS

Introduction

Our first attempt to peer into the workings of the mind was when our mum tried to get us to meditate when we were around thirteen years old. We both sat there opening one eye every couple of seconds to pull faces at each other, trying not to giggle, until our mum gave up in exasperation. Little did we know that in just a few years' time we would both be regularly practising meditation and great believers in its benefits for mental health and wellbeing.

Today, after many years of exploration both mentally and globally, together and apart, we have come to realise that our understandings of the mind and wellbeing are in harmony, despite the fact that we come at them from very different angles. Even though we are twins, our strengths and interests could not lie further apart. Fran was drawn to the arts at school and did not have much interest in 'academic' learning at all. She was deeply intrigued by human relationships and as we approached adulthood became the person that everyone and anyone would go to with their problems. After completing a psychology degree in London, a place she has called home ever since with a few trips overseas, Fran trained to become a psychotherapist specialising in Mindfulness, the perfect job for her, and one she passionately enjoys.

Jo meanwhile was considered 'academic', always with her nose in a book from a young age and ended up doing degrees in economics and accounting. With a thirst for variety and frustrating inability to decide on one set path, she ended up working for a period in not-for-profits in different parts of the world, before veering off into a financial analyst role in state government in Perth, Western Australia, where she decided to settle and have a family.

Despite being separated by thousands of miles of land and sea, we both found ourselves deeply fascinated in and frequently discussing life's roller-coaster of emotional lessons. Fran was now gaining considerable experience in the area with her client work and own professional development, and Jo's continuing curiosity meant that she was doing all she could to better understand life's emotional journey; from 10 days of agonisingly silent vipassana meditation, to reading everything that she felt could add to her knowledge. Our differences meant that we approached and understood ideas about holistic well-being from such contrasting angles that we found we could learn and grow from each other.

Increasingly one crucial idea kept popping up that we both firmly agreed upon. We feel that the focus today is too much on the physical and external, especially on our bodies in our culture and particularly for females although increasingly for males too. There's been an avalanche of diets and advice since the 70s when it was decided that being slim and attractive should be one of modern women's, and increasingly men's, main pursuits in life. But we believe this single-minded focus has been to the neglect of our mental and spiritual health. We believe what you put into your mind is as important as what you put into your body. And ultimately it is our mental and spiritual health that makes us happy and not how fabulous we look in our swimwear.

Which is why we decided it was time to create a 'mind' diet, a diet about what you put in your mind, rather than what you put in your mouth. If you have a healthy mind that you consciously direct to serve you rather than letting it run wild, you'll find that the will to achieve all the goals you desire, including the healthy body you want, will also be there.

The aim of this mind diet detox is to refresh, reinvigorate, and inspire you, and bring some peace into your life. We see it as a detox for the mind. It only requires effort for one day rather than trying to implement change every day, although as with any diet, the aim eventually is to change the way you think permanently to progress you towards a stronger, calmer mind and help you achieve your full potential.

All mind diets must be tailored specifically for you, which is why in this book we give you the ingredients and structure, and you choose the most effective route for yourself. Everyone is unique and it is up to you to choose what will work best for you. The mind diet detox is designed so that no matter how much you choose to do you can still see benefits. Any one of the ingredients will add something positively nourishing to your life. And as you play around with different variations you will find that you will start to feel more drawn to certain aspects of the diet and these will then become easier to implement into your everyday life.

Creating this Mind Diet Detox has taught us so much, and in particular how often we ourselves are still in need of a regular mind detox. We believe there is so much to learn in life and that there is always room for growth.

We hope this detox will give you at least some tools to consciously take control of your life and progress on your journey towards becoming the best, happiest version of yourself that you can possibly be!

We got there in the end Mum.

Fran and Jo

1. Mind Diet Basics

It's easier to stick to a diet if you understand how it works. This chapter tries to do that by explaining the basic beliefs that underpin the Mind Diet and provide you with some details on how this incredibly complex, bustling force we feel in our head, the mind, works.

Now we've decided there are three fundamental beliefs that will help you understand the Mind Diet. We've called them 'beliefs' because when dealing with the mind it's impossible to say what's true and what's not, as it is the mind trying to describe itself.

This means that every way of trying to describe how the mind works is only a metaphor or analogy. It can only be compared to something else. It's a bit like trying to describe the taste of beetroot to someone who has never tasted it before. You can explain as much as you like by saying what other things it tastes similar to, but you can never describe exactly what it tastes like or fully know if what you are describing is being understood in the same way by someone else.

In Psychology, the mind is described as the totality of conscious and unconscious mental processes and activities.

The Oxford Dictionary describes the mind as 'the element of a person that enables them to be aware of the world and their experiences, to think, and to feel: the faculty of consciousness and thought'.

The mind's workings can be described in so many different ways, and it might be that some descriptions resonate more with you than others; grab onto these as these are the ones that will help you the most in understanding the mind and teaching you to tame it.

1.1. We Create Our World with Our Minds

With our minds we create our own world.
Buddha

Our first fundamental belief about the mind has been repeated time and time again in many different ways throughout the history of humankind. The Buddha said it in his deceptively simple way over two thousand years ago, 'with our minds we create our own world'.

It's our belief that your mind plays a pivotal role in creating your experience of the world. It's through our minds that we try to make sense and interpret this world and our experience of it.

And in fact, in this way it can be said to create your world as it is how you feel and think about your experiences that really matters, not the actual external experience itself. Yes, of course external circumstances have an influence and impact upon you, but it's your mind that translates all these experiences into your thoughts and feelings and, for the most part, decides whether they are positive or negative.

Standing in queue for a long time or walking to work in the rain because the bus hasn't turned up are only as difficult as your thoughts make them. Frustration, annoyance and disappointment are generally feelings invented by the thoughts you have about the situation. 'This queue is taking longer than I want it to and that annoys me.' This **Self Check:** What little things do I get frustrated over? response is your mind's reaction to a situation that is neither positive or negative. It just is.

Once in a negative mood, your mind also has a nasty habit of interpreting things or even looking for things to validate its current state. For example, you've woken up in a bad mood. You look out of the window and it's raining and you think 'typical'. You go downstairs to make breakfast and remember you forgot to pick up milk yesterday so no coffee. This just increases your bad mood. You decide to leave the house early so that you can get a coffee on the way before you meet a friend but on route you get a message from them telling you they are running late due to traffic. At this point you have a choice how to respond but because you are already in a bad mood your response is 'they should have factored the traffic into their journey time and the fact they are now running late means they're ruining my day even more'. The mind's agenda here is to continue to feed the bad mood so it seeks out evidence to keep proving it. But when you pick apart what has actually happened you realise there has been no real trauma or upsetting event to keep feeding the bad mood. Rain is just a weather condition that means you might get wet. No milk means you did not have a coffee at the time you wanted one. Your friend running late means you did not meet that person at exactly the time you had previously agreed. Each of these incidents, when taken away from the negative thought process, is just an event with no negative consequence. The negative consequence (the bad mood) is only added by the thoughts that the mind creates when it translates the experience.

Charles Swindoll, the American Pastor, put it another way.

We cannot change our past…we cannot change the fact that people will act in a certain way. We cannot change the inevitable. The only thing we can do is play on the one string we have, and that is our attitude. I am convinced that life is 10% what happens to me and 90% of how I react to it.
Charles R Swindoll.

How we react to life is crucial, not only because this is one of the major determinants of our happiness, but also because we often have no or very little control over the things that happen to us. As Winston Churchill purportedly stated, 'history is simply one damned thing after another', and life can often feel like this too.

We frequently work tirelessly to try and make our lives exactly the way we want; the perfect partner, the fulfilling and financially rewarding job, the beautiful home, but as we all know things often don't turn out the way we dream about. And even if they do, they don't guarantee happiness. There are so many things outside of our control; as Malcolm Gladwell describes in his book *Outliers*, success more often than not depends upon things other than your talents and efforts, such as the environment you are born into and crucially the opportunities at the time that exist for you.

Twin Tales

Jo came to understand these concepts a little earlier than Fran. It led to rollicking arguments between us. Jo understood many of the ideas from an intellectual and rational perspective but then applied them with a lack of compassion. She judged Fran for all sorts of things, but mainly for not understanding that she could change the way she thought and reacted to things.

Fran on her side found Jo's approach harsh and was defensive, and as a student of psychology had decided she was unwilling to listen to anything that Jo had to say about the mind.
Once Fran began to understand these ideas from an emotional space, which was the only place she was ever going to learn them from, she took them on board, and really 'lived' them much better and faster than Jo. And the arguments, thank goodness, disappeared and our twin connection grew and grew.

It's important to understand that we all have our own path to follow, and we all learn in our own way in our own time. Remember, if something doesn't resonate with you, it might not be right for you at this time, but it might really work for someone else. Keep an open mind, and try not to judge others wherever they are on their path.

So, if we don't have much control over what happens to us, and our mind creates our world by translating everything into thoughts and emotions, what can we do about this?
Crucially, we do have control over how our mind interprets and responds to events. Not only can we learn to watch how our mind reacts, we can also learn to watch how we react to our mind. This then gives us a choice in how we respond.

This is an important concept as many people are unaware that they can change the way their mind reacts and thinks. Throughout our childhood and into adulthood our story is created; who we are; what we like and don't like; and with this information all our emotional habits and reactions are formed.

> *Folks are usually about as happy as they make up their minds to be.*
> Abraham Lincoln

As we get older, these habits and reactions become engrained, and can seem unchangeable, but the truth is that we have the power to change absolutely any belief or habit that originates from the mind.

This leads us on to our second fundamental belief for the Mind Diet Detox.

1.2. You are the Master of Your Mind

There is nothing more important to true growth than realising that you are not the voice of the mind - you are the one that hears it.
Michael E. Singer

You don't have to fall for everything your mind tells you. Understanding that you don't have to be the thoughts in your mind or believe everything it says can be transformative. As Michael Singer says, you are not the voice of your mind, you are the one listening to it.

By listening to your mind, rather than unconsciously following its every instruction and thought, you can gradually teach it to better serve you.
We so often mistake our moods for reality. Our minds can be such a positive force, but also unfortunately negative. For some reason we can see that other people have opinions but our mind is often only full of facts, 'you might think I look nice but I know I look awful.'

Once you start listening to your mind, you can begin changing it. By this we mean learning to respond differently to it which over time changes how it will respond to different events and situations. You start working from the inside out instead of outside in which is ultimately far easier and more within your control.

For example, you may have had a bad experience with a partner, which means that you now find it harder to trust people. So, when you first meet a potential partner, you are cold, a little distant and wary of them. Over the years it becomes a habitual reaction, you're not even aware you're doing it, and prospective partners often find it off-putting. When you

The difference between an **opinion and a fact** is that an opinion can change without new information whereas a fact cannot. You can look in the mirror in the morning and think you look awful but a few hours later you could catch a glimpse of yourself and think you look great. Nothing has changed about your appearance but your mood may have improved. Or you see yourself from a different angle and feel happier with what you see.

start to listen and become aware of your mind's reactions you realise what you are doing and that there is actually no need to be cold or distant. You've only just met the person so they're not in a position to hurt you, so why not be more open-minded, and give yourself a better chance of creating a new relationship?

Do you know some of your common mind's reactions, for example what makes you angry or frustrated and why? Do you think your mind works in a way that helps you live the life you want to live?

Self Check: Ask yourself - do I like the way my mind thinks?

There's not many of us who can answer all these questions positively. So how do we go about listening to the voice of our mind, understanding it better, and changing the way it responds?

If you don't make the time to work on creating the life you want, you're eventually going to be forced to spend a LOT of time dealing with a life you don't want.
Kevin Ngo

We can do this and change our whole experience of life through awareness.

1.3. Awareness is the Key to Mastering Your Mind

To achieve a life filled with meaning, you must figure out how to be more conscious; only then do you become the author of your own destiny.
Chopra and Tanzi

Awareness is the key to permanently changing how we respond to life, and ultimately who we are.

Our success in life (however we might define it) and happiness will depend to some extent upon how well we are able to cope with what life throws at us. By increasing our awareness we are developing a skill that will enable us to do this.

So, what do we mean by awareness?

According to the dictionary, awareness is 'the state or condition of being aware; having knowledge; consciousness.' All of these definitions work for the purpose of this book. When we talk about awareness we are talking about the ability to 'know' that we are aware in any present moment. Eckhart Tolle talks about awareness being the first stage of enlightenment. We can be consciously engaged in the present moment, talking or listening to a friend, but only once we know that we are consciously engaged in talking to our friend are we able to take control of our attention. And it's this control that gives us the key to mastering our mind.

Awareness can transform our life. Living consciously can:
- help us live life more fully in the moment,
- uncover a bigger perspective so that we can pursue what is really valuable to us and reveal what we really want from life,
- reduce or break negative emotional habits or destructive behaviours,
- open us more to love, creating stronger and deeper social connections,
- free us from caring about what other people think.

So how can it do all these things?
By being able to stay consciously aware of the thoughts in our mind we are able to see our mind's agenda and separate this from the actual, present

moment situation. This allows us to take a 'step back' and gain a bigger perspective. This can reveal so many things, such as how our mind may have fallen into automatic habitual responses that are counter-productive to our happiness, or how little things annoy us when they might not need to, or what it is we really value and want to spend our time doing.

Building awareness allows us to understand our mind better and address all these different habits and reactions. This, in turn, helps us develop resilience. By developing resilience and feeling safe within our own mind we can start to take charge of our life. Positive and negative external events will always happen but once we have mastered the skill of harnessing awareness, our ability to respond to them in a more helpful way will start to become our default setting. There is a famous saying 'pain is pain, but suffering is optional.'

This doesn't mean that we do not experience sadness or pain when someone we love passes away or we lose a relationship or job. We are supposed to experience sadness, anger and hopelessness but with awareness and compassion we do not have to suffer unnecessarily. By which we mean that by allowing the natural process of loss to occur with awareness, we are better able to move through difficult times and return to a place of acceptance.

A good way to start understanding our mind is to think about our story. Our story is all the ideas, thoughts, and opinions that we have created and built up about ourselves over the years. It's how we define ourselves. Many people define themselves by their job, or their role in their family, or by a dominant hobby that they are passionate about. When asked who we are, we might say, 'I'm a male engineer with a wife and three kids', or "I'm a mother who works part-time', or 'I'm a mature student hoping to run my own business'.

Self Check: What is my story? How would I define myself? If had to describe who I am to someone in one minute, what would I say? Focus on who you are, rather than what you do on a daily basis.

But is this who you truly are? Does this really describe your values, your hopes and dreams, your deeply unique characteristics?

Our deeper story that we have created and that is often subconscious, also tells us all sorts of things about who we are, such as what we are good at, what we fear and how we respond to certain people and events. There are often parts to this story that we tell ourselves that do not actually help us to live the life we want or help us be happy.

Twin Tales

Some of the stories that we built up when we were young were developed almost in opposition to each other as twins. Jo was considered academic and Fran arty, and neither of us could be both.

Fran integrated this story so well and expectations were set so low that she sometimes didn't put in as much effort as she could have. In one of her most critical GCSE exams, she decided that 3 hours was more than enough to complete it and decided to have a nap BEFORE STARTING. Needless to say the teacher woke her up not too long before the end, and she had to write like mad to get it all done.

Jo in contrast was considered hopeless at anything artistic, and decided for years not to even attempt anything remotely creative. Both these stories put us at a disadvantage. Fran has gradually realised that she is actually quite competent at many written and organisational type tasks and this belief has allowed her to pursue a career on her own terms. Jo now understands that everyone is creative in some way and set up her own jewellery company, creating the jewellery and brand herself.

Our stories can often lead to limiting beliefs that mean we miss out on nourishing activities (such as creative ones!) or do not feel we are capable of achieving our goals. It's important to try and understand whether your perceived weaknesses are just that, 'perceived', or whether they truly are limitations.

For example, are we using a core belief (see blue box) about ourselves to underpin our understanding of things that happen to us or direct us in a certain way?

It may be that you decided early on that you are not good in big groups, and people are not going to want to talk to you. This belief could have developed as a small child in your first days at school, which you found (not surprisingly) over-whelming. Over the years, this belief becomes engrained and you never make any effort in big groups because you deeply believe that you are not able to, and that no one will respond positively.

A **Core Belief** in psychology is a central belief a person has about themselves such as 'I am unlovable', 'I am strong' or 'I am weak'.
These types of belief are usually created in chidhood or adolescence and when activated are experienced as absolute truths and unlikely to be challenged. One way to detect these types of belief is to notice the thoughts accompanied by a strong emotion that do not shift in the face of contradictory evidence.
For example; The core belief would be 'I am unattractive'. Whenever someone gives you a compliment you are able to reject it as meaningless by various other beliefs that you have developed to validate your core belief. These could range from 'they are only being polite' to 'they are lying'.

Habitual responses and core beliefs like these can inhibit our lives and remove spontaneity (and freedom) as we react in habitual ways without ever trying to change. Your mind will also often interpret events to validate and deepen your core beliefs. So, continuing with the example above, if the person leading a big group does not directly address you, you see this as confirmation that nobody actually wants to speak to you, although it is much more likely that the person has noticed that you are shy and does not want to intimidate you.

These types of beliefs are usually created in childhood or adolescence and when activated are experienced as absolute truths and unlikely to be challenged. One way to detect these types of beliefs is to notice the thoughts accompanied by a strong emotion that do not shift in the face of contradictory evidence.

For example, another common core belief is 'I am not good enough'. This can impact all areas of your life but often manifests itself in your work environment. Whether it's a job interview or going for a promotion this core belief can prevent you from even attempting these things and when you do, it can belittle and criticise every thing you say and do, making you feel terrible and therefore confirming itself. This core belief can persist despite countless evidence to the contrary, to the extent that some people feel like an 'imposter' in their role (even though they have been chosen for it), hiding a deep-rooted fear that everyone will find out one day that they are not actually good enough.

Self Check: Can you think of any core beliefs you have about yourself?

Once we become more aware of our mind and its reactions, we are then in a position to recognise whether our understanding of the situation is based in the present moment reality or if the present moment reality has been woven into a story created by our mind that needs validating.

Another common habit of the mind is to resist the place we are in, wishing things were better or different. But we are trying to change something that already is, so by learning to accept the past and the present we allow for another, more helpful response to the situation. Resistance only creates more difficulty by not allowing change in any direction, so if we can remove resistance we then have the space to create a thought path that is more solution focused and helpful rather than denial based.

Scientists have recently been making many discoveries that help us understand our mind, and our habits and behaviours and how we can change them. It used to be believed that the brain developed during childhood and then remained essentially the same throughout adulthood.

It is now understood however that the brain can change at any point in one's life (see blue box on neuroplasticity). Habits and behaviours are hardwired into our brain through repetition and become automatic. By changing the way we respond to our mind we are creating new neural pathways. So we are actually changing the way our mind thinks! And with regular upkeep these new neural pathways will stay and the way we react will change forever.

Neuroplasticity is the ability of the brain to change throughout one's life. The discovery that the brain can create new axons and dendrites right up to the very last years of life has had significant implications for theories of memory and learning as well as for conditions like dementia and sufferers of brain damage. When you learn new things, and change your habits your actual brain changes as new neural pathways are formed. You can promote neuroplasticity by exposing yourself to new experiences or learning new skills.

So how do we become more aware to better understand and change our minds to help us live the life we want to live?

There are many tools to help with awareness, many of which we have harnessed in the Mind Diet Detox.

Mindfulness and meditation are two very popular awareness tools. Mindfulness is about becoming more aware of your thoughts. It teaches you how to witness the thoughts in your mind, and then respond from a calmer, more rational space. Mediation also trains you to witness your thoughts without reaction, rather than fully immersing into every thought without question. You'll learn more about these in the next chapter.

There are also different types of therapies to help you recognise unhelpful habits and thought patterns, such as Cognitive Behavioural Therapy.

How does **Cognitive Behavioural Therapy** work? It reveals your thought patterns and allows you to challenge unhelpful ones and develop new, more helpful ways of thinking. The approach is based on a combination of basic principles from behavioural and cognitive psychology and is 'problem focused' and 'action orientated'. It has proven to be very effective with phobias and anxiety disorders such as OCD.

All the ingredients in the Mind Diet Detox have been built on these beliefs, and developed to help increase your awareness and begin to gently guide your mind to better serve you.

And because every mind is unique to the person who owns it our Mind Diet Detox is as much about your exploration as it is about us giving you the tools. Our hope is that by offering you guidance and giving you a framework to explore yourself safely within, you will find a path that works for you.

> *By spending time in silence, you begin to realise that no matter what the scenery is, you are painting it. You have always painted it. In the past you did it unconsciously, randomly, chaotically. Now you consciously create a masterpiece that influences your destiny and the destiny of others.*
> Anonymous

Ultimately, the aim of the Mind Diet Detox is to gradually and simply introduce habits and practices into your life that progress you on your journey to being the best you and reaching your highest potential!

2. Detox Ingredients

So, what does a Mind Detox look like? In an increasingly anxiety driven culture everything in our ingredients list below is designed to help you on your journey to a calmer, more contented mind. Even doing the detox once can start to help you feel more positive and motivated.

We have designed this diet so that you can choose when and how much you would like to participate. If the diet is to work at its best, then finding what works for you specifically is important. For example, some people are naturally more motivated when they wake up and find it easy to do meditation in the morning, whilst others prefer to do it later in the day. According to researchers at University College London, habits are formed by context dependent repetition, which means repeating the same action in the same situation. So the more structured your diet and the more regularly you do it, the more likely your new habits are to stick.

Having researched this diet over the past couple of years with a variety of people from Fran's psychotherapy practice as well as friends and family, we have found that people use it and benefit from it in different ways.
For some, doing the Mind Detox every now and again is really helpful in re-grounding them and reminding them where they have gone off track. This could be as simple as noticing how much reliance we place on our phones, tablets or computers and how liberating it is to take a break away from this constant bombardment on our attention.
For others, they found that doing the Mind Detox on a regular basis, once a week or fortnight is the best way to gain long term benefits and change habits permanently.
Others have preferred to do the Mind Detox on demand, when they feel they are starting to slip back into old habits or feel the need for a mind reinvigoration.
Many have also found they naturally maintain some of the practices after

the diet is over. Activities like daily affirmations and maintaining a gratitude list have proved popular and easy to do at the beginning and end of the day.

This chapter will give you information on all the ingredients that will go into your diet and what you're going to do with them. Don't worry though, there are further instructions when you set up your diet plan on exactly how to use each of the ingredients.

The Six Detox Ingredients

Ingredient 1: Self-Awareness
Ingredient 2: Meditation
Ingredient 3: Self-Nourishment
Ingredient 4: Self-Care
Ingredient 5: Affirmations and Gratitude
Ingredient 6: Food, Exercise and Sleep

Ingredient 1: Self-Awareness

To achieve a life filled with meaning, you must figure out how to be more conscious; only then do you become the author of your own destiny.
Deepak Chopra

Self-awareness is the capacity for introspection and being aware of what is going on in the mind and body. It's so easy to get lost in worries about the future, or stories from the past, or to mindlessly react to certain events in the same ways we've always done.

Self-awareness helps us be the best person we can be by allowing us to become more actively aware of what we are thinking, saying and doing. It is about being in the present moment, being open to life to actively feel it and being able to see the unhelpful past stories that can translate all that we do and all that happens to us. As Deepak Chopra says, 'awareness contains the power to transform your world.'

For example, you have a lot on your mind and you're feeling stressed. Your partner does something that annoys you; it can be something as simple as putting a kitchen implement away in a different place to usual, but because you're stressed you react unconsciously, snapping at your partner who then snaps back at you.
It's amazing how these insignificant incidents can then escalate. The whole day is spent with you taking small swipes at each other and you both spend the day feeling slightly bothered. These sorts of interactions can then become habitual and happen regularly for years and years until you just accept that this is how your relationship works.

Awareness can help you in so many ways in this situation. Being aware of your own state of mind means that you can take action before you get too stressed rather than leaving it to a point where you begin to lose control. You begin to gain an understanding of your reactions with awareness and can stop yourself acting unconsciously in a way that is just going to cause more problems.

Awareness can also broaden your perspective and allow you to see the bigger picture, so that you can more easily see the futility of spending a day in mindless bickering. So instead of seeing your partner's actions as thoughtless, stupid or purposely annoying you are able to see that your own stress could be playing a part in your response too. You learn to take responsibility for your part in any given situation.

So often this type of negative or unhelpful thinking goes on in our minds and we don't even realise it. We just assume we have no choice over our reactions but when we become aware of our thoughts and what is motivating them we are able to see far more clearly, and we can challenge the initial reaction and respond from a calmer, less ego motivated place.

But how do we become more aware? Meditation is obviously a fantastic tool for developing self-awareness but that will be discussed in more detail in the next ingredient. Mindful check-ins are also a great way to start learning to observe yourself and increase your awareness on a regular basis, whilst a daily intention can help set your focus for the day.

Mindful Check-ins
The check-ins are designed to help you start to notice what is happening in your mind when you leave it unattended and begin to see how much time you actually spend in the present moment. It involves noting down what you are doing, thinking and feeling on a regular basis.
By setting alarms you can catch your mind off-guard and see where it has gone. Are you engaged with the task at hand or are you thinking about something else? If you are thinking about something else, is it creating an emotion in the body?

As you start to become more familiar with your mind and where it wanders off to you start to recognize which thoughts are helpful and based in the present moment reality and which thoughts are unhelpful and can be discarded. You start to recognise when the feeling should be taken seriously and when it is just your mind creating a scenario that isn't actually happening or helpful. And more often than not you notice that if you are in the present moment, unless something dramatic is happening, your emotions are pretty calm and neutral.

You may find when you start doing your mindful check-ins that quite often you won't notice a strong emotion or physical sensation. The more in sync you are with yourself the more likely your emotions will be in sync with whatever your current situation is and if your current situation is neutral, like washing up, than your emotions will be too.

The best way to do a mindful check-in is to set an alarm on your phone, watch or clock. You can do this 5-6 times a day, or even every hour if you feel like this is achievable. There are also apps that you can download onto your device that will set off a mindfulness alarm (a Tibetan bowl or chime for example) such as MindBell (see the Mind Diet Pantry for further information).

When the alarm goes off stop whatever you are doing and take 3 slow, deep breaths. Whilst you are breathing notice what you were doing when the alarm went off, what you were thinking and notice what you are feeling emotionally. Jot these down on your daily diet plan whenever possible.

It's really interesting to see at the end of the day how often you were actually engaged in the present moment and how often your mind had drifted off somewhere else. It can also be a good reminder that all thoughts and emotions are transient and come and go on a regular basis.

Set an Intention

Setting an intention for the day helps you to really focus on one area or goal in your life and move towards changing or achieving it. Intentions can vary widely from a general one such as 'I will listen with my full attention to everyone I talk to today' to a more specific one such as 'I will not snap at my son today.' We, at the Mind Diet, often set a daily or weekly intention such as 'I will be kind' or 'I will stay focused.' Intentions really help you remain pointed in the right direction, and when you are tempted to veer off course the intention can bring you back.

It's good to put a bit of thought into your intention and make sure it really is something you are interested in and want to achieve. When you have a clear intention being able to return to it throughout the day really helps you to focus on what is important and helps you make decisions and choices based on this information.

For example; your intention is 'I will eat healthily today', when a piece of cake is offered or the smell of your favourite burger drifts by you are able to revert to your intention which will guide you back onto the path you have chosen. Limiting your intention to one per day means that firstly, you don't get bogged down in having to decide which intention to follow and secondly it allows you to start a fresh intention each day, making it easier to stick to.

To help you set your intention we've created an Intentions List in the Detox Supplements. However, intentions are as unique as the individual and we encourage you, wherever possible, to use these just as a guide and to come up with your own.

Twin Tales

Enhancing awareness can lead to some interesting insights into yourself that you may have been entirely unaware of before (although more often than not the knowledge is there; it's just deeply hidden or you've employed some clever strategies to ignore it).

Although Fran and I are very different in obvious ways, with awareness we have come to realise that we'd also developed some similar, not very helpful behaviours.

Both of us were quite hedonistic as teenagers and young adults, and we derived a lot of our self-worth from the approval of the opposite sex. At times, this led to competition between us for male attention, and our self-esteem was built upon unstable ground that was prone to collapsing depending on who won!

With increasing awareness and gradually learning from wellbeing experts, we have come to understand, as Deepak Chopra says, that you alone should be the judge of your self-worth. Handing over how you feel about yourself to others is a recipe for disaster and likely to lead to a yo-yoing self-esteem. It's insights like these that have made us realise that prioritising awareness really is invaluable.

Ingredient 2: Meditation

The aim of meditation is to transform the mind. Every one of us has a mind and every one of us can work on it.
Matthieu Riccard

Meditation is a practice that gives balance physically, emotionally and mentally and is an important aspect of our Mind Detox. You don't have to practice for hours every day, even just a couple of minutes can make a difference to how you see and feel about the world around you.

Today, people are using meditation to treat a variety of ailments including anxiety, stress, and depression. The "deep rest" meditation gives a person has been shown, amongst other things to:

- Dissolve stress and improve the ability to relaxImprove self-esteem
- Enable clearer decision-making
- Reduce blood pressure
- Help people quit smoking, conquer drug and alcohol addictions
- Reduce symptoms of pre-menstrual syndrome and menopause

We believe however, that meditation can do much more than just help you relax and de-stress. Becoming aware of your thoughts and being more present in the moment allows you to see your own situation with much more clarity and wisdom, and to more consciously direct your thinking and your life in a direction that is beneficial to you and those around you. Ultimately it can bring you to a closer understanding of your own true nature, what it is that makes you truly and deeply happy and allow you to live life to its fullest in your own unique way.

Meditation is a personal practice and it is important that you find one that works for you. For some people guided meditation gives them an anchor in the present and something to return to when the mind wanders off, whereas for others guided meditation can feel like an intrusion. Take some time to find out what works for you. We personally both switch between guided and non-guided, we like the variety.
There are so many different options for meditation and if you go online

you can find hundreds of free meditation sites. We have picked a few here that we have used personally and found really helpful but please feel free to use your own if ours don't take your fancy. There are also further tips on meditation in the Mind Diet Pantry. You may already have your own meditation practice in which case please just drop this into the diet where you would normally fit it into your day.

Body Scan Meditation

1. Find somewhere quiet to lie down comfortably with your legs straight and uncrossed and your arms lying gently by your side, palms facing up or down. In yoga this is called 'corpse pose.'
2. Once you are lying comfortably start to notice your breath by moving your awareness to the physical sensation of breathing. This could be your belly rising and falling, your chest rising and falling or the sensation of breath coming in and out of your nose, whichever one of these physical sensations is the strongest.
3. Follow your own breath gently for 5-6 breaths. There is no need to force the breath, you can just follow your own gentle rhythm. Then move your awareness to your toes. See if you can 'experience' that part of your body. Then slowly start to make your way back up to your head moving through each part of your body from the soles of your feet, heels, ankles, shins and calves, knee caps, thighs, pelvis and groin, belly and back, chest and spine, shoulders, biceps, elbows, forearms and then hands and fingers, then back up the neck, through your face and up to the top of your skull.
4. As you move through each area try and notice if you are holding any tension. If you are gently breath into the area and release any tensed muscles.
5. You will also notice that your mind may wander off to 'think' about something else like 'what to have for dinner later' or 'remembering the car needs a service'. When this happens gently bring it back to the part of the body you are trying to focus on. Continue to do this until you reach your head.

Teardrop meditation

1. Find somewhere quiet to sit. You can choose to sit on a chair or in the lotus position with a cushion on the floor placing your hands either in your lap with the palms facing up or on your knees.
2. When you are seated comfortably gently bring your focus to the breath and start to follow it. You can do this for a few breaths to bring yourself into a calmer space.
3. Once you are feeling more focused take a long, slow inhale. When you reach the top of the inhale pause for a second and silently count 1.
4. Then slowly exhale all the way to the bottom of the breath and slowly back up to the top of the inhale. At the top of the inhale pause again and silently count 2.
5. Repeat this process until you have reached 10 exhale-inhale breaths.
6. Then slowly exhale all the way to the bottom of the breath and pause. You will repeat the same process as above but this time starting each breath from the bottom of the exhale. We call this the teardrop meditation because when we do this we picture each inhale-exhale as a teardrop and then we flip the image when we reverse the breathing.

Inner-Outer Senses

This meditation aims to help bring you into the present and become aware of the differences between the inner and outer worlds that we all live in.

1. Prepare as usual for your meditation.
2. Close your eyes and focus on your body. Start from the top and do a quick sweep down noticing any sensations and where they are in your body.
3. Move to focusing on your breathing, and any other sensations if they pop up.
4. Now switch to focusing on the sounds you can hear around you. Really listen. Notice any sense of touch, the clothes on your skin, where your body is touching the chair, bed or floor. Can you smell or taste anything?
5. Now switch back to focusing on your breath, and any feelings inside your body.
6. Switch between the outer world of noises, smells, tastes, and touch, and

the inner world of sensations.

7. If thoughts pop up, that's ok, acknowledge them but move back to focusing on your inner or outer world as gently as possible.

To really help to disengage from those thoughts, it can sometimes be helpful to try and focus on two of the outer world senses at the same time, for example what you can hear and the feel of your clothes on a certain area of your body. This often helps to pull your mind back to the present.

If meditation is something you have tried and found hard that is absolutely fine, we do encourage you to try again. Think of it as a workout for the mind; the first few times you go to the gym or try and run it hurts and it can be really hard but over time it gets easier. It is the same with meditation.

You are activating parts of the brain that you don't often consciously use and it can take a little time before it begins to feels comfortable. You are dropping out of 'doing mode' and into 'being mode' and this can sometimes take a little bit of effort and persuasion on the part of your mind.

If you feel it's really not for you however, replace meditation with solitary exercise (jogging, cycling, walking, yoga, stretching etc.). Try and focus fully on your breath and body whilst exercising in a mindful way. Notice how your body feels as you move it and really try and focus on which of your senses are activated and how. For example, when running outside you may notice the warm/cool air on the parts of your body that are exposed and the smell of different parts of your route. You will also see and hear different things as you run past. Every time your mind drifts, bring it back to the present moment using your body and breath.

Twin Tales

We once had a bizarre argument about meditating. Neither of us had been meditating for long, but Jo had been meditating for longer so she thought she knew more. We were talking about where you feel that sense of yourself, your thinking place, when you attain a good meditative state, and Jo said it was definitely in the head. Fran said no it was in the heart, and we argued about it. It seems funny now; what a thing to argue over! But also so very revealing.

Fran works so often from the heart, whilst Jo is always trying to figure everything out from the head. It means Fran is warmer, more able to feel her emotions, but also more vulnerable with a more penetrable self-esteem.

Whereas Jo can rationalise herself out of things that are bad for her, and has a sturdier self-assurance, people do not warm to her in the same way, and sometimes she finds it hard to feel the emotions of life.

In the end though, it's always about balance in life, the yin and the yang, there is never a wrong or a right. It's up to you to find the right way for you at any given moment, to work from the head or the heart.

Ingredient 3: Self-Nourishment

Life gives you plenty of time to do whatever you want to do if you stay in the present moment.
Deepak Chopra

We so often fill our days up with mindless distraction or 'busyness', activities that are not really achieving anything but that can distract us for minutes or even hours at a time. These activities often give us instant gratification (although frequently at a later cost) or have the effect of numbing the mind. This ingredient is about finding nourishing activities that have longer-term benefits and really give you a deeper satisfaction.
We've compiled a list of what we see as nourishing activities below but if you want to add your own activity, one that you know will really give you long-lasting satisfaction, please do so.

* Spend time in nature
* Do something for someone else
* Declutter/ Simplify Your life
* Do something creative
* Connect with others

Spend time in nature
Of all the paths you take in life, make sure a few of them are dirt.
John Muir

Spending time in nature allows us to reconnect with our roots. Before the advent of agriculture that led to settled societies, we lived nomadically, deeply immersed in nature, and using its resources only for our immediate needs.
But in today's society, where most of us live in built up cities and buy our groceries from a store, we see nature as separate from us and have forgotten the importance of our connection to the land.
As Alan Watts, who wrote one of the first best-selling Western books on Buddhism says, 'we do not come into this world; we come out of it, as leaves from a tree.' We are as much a part of nature as those leaves.

Even just five minutes in fresh air can give you a much-needed boost and reinvigorate your soul. And if you do have access to nature in a more amenable climate, then walking barefoot on grass or sand really reconnects you to the earth. City dwellers can find a park or even a street bench and just spend five minutes outside, listening to the sounds of the city and noticing the breeze, or lack of, on their face.

Do something for someone else
It is in giving that I connect with others, with the world and with the divine.
Isabel Allende

An interesting research study conducted by social psychologist Liz Dunn and her colleagues at the University of British Columbia demonstrated how people gain a greater sense of happiness when they give to others rather than themselves.
The researchers gave students an envelope with money in and told them they could either spend it on themselves or spend it on someone else. Those who spent it on someone else reported greater feelings of happiness than those who chose to spend it on themselves.

If you choose this activity, it's obviously not just about spending money on others but also helping others in any capacity. You could offer to babysit for a friend or cook extra food for your elderly neighbor next door. You could spend an evening with a family member who you know is usually alone or invite them round for dinner. There are so many things that we can do for others and even the smallest gesture can make someone else's day, as well as our own.

Saying thank-you to someone is another simple way of passing on a sense of goodness and joy. Think of someone from your past who helped you through a difficult time or gave you something you really need. Find them and thank them telling them why. You can do this face-to-face or by phone or letter. A handwritten note can be just as special as a face to face thank you. Or think of someone who is often over looked and not thanked (a bus driver, shop keeper, parent, friend, helpful work colleague or receptionist) and thank them for their contribution to your life. Or prepare and send a care package to someone you love. After all, who doesn't love getting a parcel in the post.

De-clutter/ Simplify your life

The question of what you want to own is actually the question of how you want to live your life.
Marie Kondo

Over time we all accumulate stuff, some of it more 'precious' than others. But what it all has in common is our attachment to it. We often don't even know what we have but we don't throw it away. We keep things 'just in case...', whether it's that little black dress that we WILL fit into again or that broken radio/toaster/lamp that we will fix one day.

Holding on to 'stuff' can impact us psychologically. That dress we want to fit back into is a constant reminder that we think we are too big as we are and we will be happier only when we lose weight. That broken device stops us from buying a new one because it's a waste of money and our space becomes cluttered with things that we cannot use. This can also block us emotionally from moving forward and trying new things. We end up sticking to the familiar, however unworkable, as it is safe, and the unknown is just that, unknown, and therefore scary and should be avoided.

But life cannot improve without change and something as simple as de-cluttering your personal space can help make that first vital step towards change easier. You can start with a kitchen cupboard or clothes drawer in your bedroom. Remove everything and put it in a pile. Then work steadily through each piece, taking the time to look at it and ask questions like:

- Do I need this?
- Do I use/wear this?
- When did I last use/wear this?
- Do I even like this?
- Why am I keeping this?

And be harsh, if the answer to more than 1 of these questions is negative then give it to charity or to someone in need, recycle it or bin it.
In the same vein, we often fill our life up with unnecessary activities that drain us rather than fulfill us or help us achieve our dreams. We have put together some easy ways to simplify your life right now so that you can

spend more time focusing on the stuff that is really important to you:

- Evaluate your commitments: prioritise your commitments and practise saying no. You don't have to accept every invitation you are offered.
- Assess your daily habits: write down a brief list of what you would like to do on a daily basis (exercise, spend quality time with family, meditate etc.). Then write down a list of what you actually spend your day doing. How closely do the lists match? Is there a way you can make your days a little more filled with what you'd like to be doing?
- Audit your social media: unfollow, unfriend and delete unused apps – (this is a great one to do but should probably be done on a non-diet day so you don't get tempted to start scrolling through your social media or using apps!)
- Practise being less busy; try single-tasking rather than always multi-tasking and leave a whole day or even an entire weekend unplanned.

Do something creative
Creativity is intelligence having fun.
Einstein

Creativity has been proven in numerous studies to be good for both your mental and your physical health. Creating art, playing music, dancing, writing, decorating or even re-arranging your bedroom can relieve stress and anxiety, and reinvigorate and inspire you.

In this age of abundant information, with on-demand TV, adverts everywhere, social media and of course the Internet, we can spend so much time consuming information and entertainment we forget to take part. Taking a break from this onslaught and spending time in the process of creation calms your mind and allows you to connect more deeply with your own desires and self.
For this activity, spend at least half an hour doing something creative, and remember it doesn't have to be to a professional level. Just let yourself go!

Ideas:
- Painting

- Playing an instrument
- Singing
- Dancing
- Writing
- Interior decorating
- Cooking
- Crafting
- Gardening
- Woodwork
- Knitting/Crocheting/Tapestry

Connect with others

Each contact with a human being is so rare, so precious, one should preserve it.
Anais Anin

The breadth, depth and meaning of our social relationships are actually the best predictors of our happiness. Research has shown that possessing strong social bonds can actually improve your physical health, and conversely, isolation can lead to health problems.

This activity is about spending quality time with friends or family. Make sure you spend the time fully engaged with them (and not multi-tasking) and ensure you spend at least half the time listening to them rather than talking. Being fully there for someone and listening to them without judgement is one of the best gifts you can give. As is often said, listening is an act of kindness.

And you don't have to be face to face; a Skype or telephone call can be just as effective as sitting down with someone. And remember to make time for them; we so often call the ones we love when we are walking to the shops or driving somewhere, hands free of course. Make sure communication is the main event and try not to multi-task.

And if you don't have strong social connections then joining a weekly group can help provide the regular interaction with others that you need. We haven't listed any options here as the choices will be so varied and there will be things happening locally to you that we don't know about so keep an eye open when out shopping or look online. Think about what you are interested in and see if there are any groups or clubs you can join.

Ingredient 4: Self-Care

You yourself, as much as anybody in the entire universe, deserve your love and affection.
Buddha

Something we often forget to do for ourselves is something nice. We tend to think that doing something nice for ourselves is spoilt or indulgent and therefore should be avoided or is reserved for special occasions. What we don't realise is that doing something nice for ourselves is also a way of developing self-compassion and reducing stress and even loneliness. It's a way of saying 'thank-you' to ourselves for being there. Developing self-compassion means that we start to develop a friendship with ourselves and so spending time alone becomes more enjoyable and we feel less lonely.

When was the last time you took a few minutes to look after yourself? There is a difference between 'treating yourself' and avoiding yourself or numbing difficult emotions. We want you to be careful not to fall into the bad habits or avoidance traps you may already have in your life. These tend to involve activities that don't require our participation in the same way as a nourishing treat.

For example; some people will find that whenever they want a treat they will turn to the biscuit tin or switch on the television. For others it's opening that bottle of wine or having that cigarette. These are not treats in the nutritious sense and this ingredient is all about nutritious treats (see the list below).

How do you tell the difference? Well, when the treat is over you will feel better about yourself, you will also notice that the positive experience continues even after you have finished. Usually, the biscuit is only enjoyable as long as you are eating it, the tv show is only interesting when you are watching it. But a nutritious treat will leave you feeling good and you will reap the benefits even after you have finished. Now every ingredient in our diet is a different way of developing self-care but this one is specifically about treating yourself in a nourishing way.

We are not asking you to go out and spend a fortune, it can be as simple as a candle lit bath or time with your favourite book. It can be allowing yourself that extra 20 minutes in bed. Whatever you choose to do make sure it is something that you wouldn't normally allow for yourself and for once give yourself permission, permission to be kind to yourself.

By spending quality time with yourself you are starting a really healthy habit that over time decreases feelings of loneliness and disappointment and helps develop that much needed friend in your mind.

It also decreases our need to seek validation externally from others because, by being kind to ourselves, we are in essence telling ourselves that we are 'good enough' and we 'deserve to be treated well.' Or at the very least that we can enjoy time spent alone and we do not need to avoid it.

Self-Care Ideas:
- Curl up somewhere comfy and read a book
- Walk somewhere beautiful in nature (try not to have any other goals like a fitness goal, just focus on the walk)
- Invest in a nourishing facial or reviving massage
- Lie somewhere comfortable (in the yoga savasana pose if desired) and listen to beautiful, calming music
- Do a slow, relaxing yoga session (such as yin or restorative yoga) or stretching session
- Take a favourite walk with your dog
- Curl up with your pet and reap the benefits of the unconditional love they provide
- Play games with your children
- Sit down with an old photo album and remember fond memories
- Take a nap
- Burn your favourite scented candle and relax
- Watch sunset or sunrise
- Go treat yourself and get a manicure or pedicure
- Take a long, candle-lit bath
- Curl up and listen to your favourite podcast with nothing else to do
- Listen to some music from the happiest period in your life, one that brings back great memories
- Put on some freshly laundered clothes, straight from the tumble dryer or washing line
- If you have any old toys, for example, Lego or Playmobile, get these out and enjoy being a kid again

Ingredient 5: Affirmations and Gratitude

I don't have to chase extraordinary moments to find happiness- it is right in front of me if I'm paying attention and practicing gratitude.
Brene Brown

Both affirmations and gratitude exercises can help steer your mind onto a more positive course. Unfortunately, once a negative thought has taken hold, your mind has a habit of trying to bring up every other negative thought related to it keeping you in a cycle of negative thinking, and you can often find yourself unconsciously submerged in a pit of negativity. By consciously repeating affirmations, and acknowledging what is good in your life, you can direct yourself away from this state and towards a more positive one.

Affirmations

An affirmation is a short, powerful statement that helps you focus your mind in a positive direction, for example; 'May I be happy, May I be healthy'.
We have around 60,000 thoughts a day with the majority of these being repetitive or unhelpful because of the natural negative bias in our minds, which is why we are still alive as a species today, but in a world full of perceived threats our reptile brain is having a field day, seeing threats in all corners.

So, affirmations are a great way of directing our thoughts onto a more positive path and can be incredibly powerful. Science has proven that affirmations, if repeated often enough, can actually alter the brain's neural pathways, changing the way we think permanently and helping us shift our bias towards a more positive frame of mind. This does not mean we no longer perceive any threats, just that we are less likely to worry or think about the ones that aren't dangerous.

The best way to use affirmations is to repeat them aloud and confidently when you wake up, and at various points throughout the day. We realise this may not always be something you can do however, (without attracting strange looks) so you can also just repeat them in your head. Just try to make sure you really focus on the words as you do and don't just repeat them mindlessly.

It's very important that you choose the affirmation that is right for you and your particular circumstances at the time. There is a list of Affirmations to help you in the Detox Supplements categorized under the different emotional states they inspire. But of course you can always choose your own.

For the Mind Detox you can choose up to 4 affirmations. Repeat them at your Mindful Check In or whenever you need throughout the day.

Gratitude

When you acknowledge and are grateful for whatever you have, it allows more to be drawn to you and changes the way you experience life.
Oprah Winfrey.

Practising gratitude can have an enormous impact on your life. Research at Harvard University has shown that if you practice saying three things you are grateful for every morning (and they have to be different things each day) you can start to change from having a pessimist outlook on life to an optimistic one. And it doesn't matter how long you've been a pessimist for! It's also been shown to boost life satisfaction, strengthen your relationships with self and others, and improve compassion and your desire to help others.

Importantly, gratitude can be transformative because it gives you perspective. It's so easy to get caught up in the little annoyances and frustrations of life so that you end up forgetting all the good things that exist, and the wonderful things you come across every day, no matter how small. When you stop and take stock you start to notice things such as the sun shining for the first time in months, the seasons changing, the colour of the sky on a beautiful day, people you love, a roof over your head, your favourite food being served at your local café, a happy dog in the park, a new flower opening up for the first time and ultimately being alive to experience it all. These things generally go unnoticed in the distracted mind but when mindfully observed can bring immense joy and gratitude.

There are several ways to practice gratitude and you can decide which one works for you from the list below.

Gratitude Exercises
Gratitude Lists
These can either be done daily or weekly, by experience or person, in detail or list form. You can choose how you record your gratitude lists but handwritten in a little notebook is our personal preference. Having somewhere that is easy to access and specifically for gratitude allows you to return to your previous thoughts and reminds you of all the things you are grateful for at a glance.

A Gratitude Jar
This should be positioned somewhere prominent in your home or workplace so that you gain residual gratitude every time you walk past. Once a day pop in a small piece of paper with what you are grateful for that day. At the end of the week or month you can sit down and read these and remind yourself of all the little things that made your week or month. We so often forget all the good things that have happened to us over the last week or month!

A Complaints/Gratitude list
Spend a day writing down every gripe and complaint you have and at the end of the day sit down and write down something that you are grateful for beside each complaint. This not only shows you how much time we spend thinking about negative things but allows you to even out your negative thinking with more positive thinking.

Ingredient 6: Food, Exercise and Sleep

Take care of your body. It's the only place you have to live.
Jim Rohn

Diet, exercise and sleep are fundamental to our wellbeing and whilst these ingredients aren't the focus of the Mind Detox they should underpin the routine for the day.

We're just going to provide you with some basic information here, as there is so much available out there on how much and what you should be eating, and what's best for you in regards to diet, exercise and sleep. Many of you will have routines that already work but for those who don't, here are some guidelines to consider when putting your diet together.

The food you eat can be either the safest and most powerful form of medicine or the slowest form of poison.
Ann Wigmore

In terms of how much you should be eating, women should be aiming for around 1500-2000 calories per day and men 2000-2500 calories per day. However, this is obviously dependent on your size and height and whether you have any special dietary requirements already in place.

What your daily menu consists of is up to you but food is a vital source of nutrition and energy so what we put into our body is really important. As a general rule, eat as many wholefoods as possible (foods that haven't been processed or refined and are unaltered from their natural state), eat a wide variety of nourishing foods - and the more colourful your food the better it is! Try to limit foods high in saturated fats (biscuits, cakes, chips etc.), and those containing a lot of salt or sugar such as junk food.

The easiest way to eat healthily on the day is to plan your meals and snacks beforehand; buy lots of beautiful fruit and vegetables, and make sure you have some healthy snacks handy for any mid-afternoon or evening cravings.

So how much exercise should you be doing? The World Health Organisation recommends that 18-64 year olds should be aiming for 150 minutes of moderate-intensity aerobic physical activity throughout the week or at least 75 minutes of vigorous-intensity aerobic physical activity per week (or an equivalent combination of moderate and vigorous intensity activity). They suggest that aerobic activity should be performed in bouts of at least 10 minutes duration. The activities you pick are up to you and again, if you have a fitness routine that works for you then continue using this on the detox day.

Sleep is the single most effective thing we can do to reset our brain and body health each day.
Matthew Walker

Everyone knows that eating well is good for you and that exercise is important. We are now also finding out the true benefits of sleep on our health. The recommended amount of sleep for an adult is between 7-9 hours per night, which may sound like a lot but the research is out there suggesting that even losing 1 hour of sleep a night can be quite detrimental to your health and wellbeing.

Good sleeping habits have so many benefits. Sleeping well has been proven to:
- improve memory
- sharpen attention and help you think more clearly
- improve your ability to focus
- reduce stress levels
- improve the immune system
- help with weight issues
- helps us remain rational and logical

Sleep impacts every aspect of our lives, from our health to our appearance to our productivity. So getting into a good sleep routine can have a huge impact on every area of your life. But we also recognise that not everyone has the luxury of going to bed at night and sleeping happily through until morning, so finding time to nap is a great way to boost your hours.

We've put together some tips that the experts recommend in order to help you sleep well:

- Try to make your bedroom a peaceful place, and only use your bed for sleep or sex.
- Try to keep your sleeping and waking times as regular as possible in order to train your biological clock.
- You should eat a good 2-3 hours before bedtime but not a very heavy meal (and avoid foods containing tyramine such as bacon, avocado, nuts, soy sauce and red wine, which can keep you awake).
- Light exercise, such as a gentle walk, before bedtime is good, but intense exercise should be avoided.
- Try and avoid bright lights, such as electronic devices of all kinds, right before bedtime as this may confuse the circadian rhythm.
- Avoid excessive alcohol consumption before bedtime (although alcohol initially acts as a sedative, it is a stimulant and will generally result in a bad night's sleep).
- A peaceful practice such as meditation or reading before bedtime can help you get to sleep quicker.

Below are a list of 7 Extra Tips we've put together to help you on your way to getting the rest, food and sleep you need.

1. Drink a large glass of water before every meal (and drink lots throughout the day).
2. Eat a real breakfast; it's the best way to start your day.
3. Try and eat dinner before 7pm so your digestive system has time to work before going to bed – don't go to bed on a full stomach.
4. Make sure you have enough time to enjoy the food you are eating and try to focus on eating without other distractions.
5. Aim for at least 30 minutes of exercise or movement per day.
6. Aim for at least 7-9 hours of sleep per night or a combination of night-time sleeping and naps.
7. Try and be washed and ready for bed at least 30 minutes before turning your light out, this helps your body move naturally towards relaxation and avoids those bright bathroom lights that will deceive the body into thinking it's daytime again!

3. Detox Instructions

To get the most out of your Mind Detox try and find a day when you are completely free from major commitments such as large social events. We also suggest that you refrain from certain things such as television, social media, alcohol and other toxic substances.

It's very important that you do a little preparation the day before. We've been doing this diet ourselves for a while and have found that doing a little prep the day before really helps you engage more fully and enjoy the process. We've also been using this diet within Fran's psychotherapy practice and the results have been incredibly positive. Clients report increased levels of awareness, positive feelings and a sense of calm and autonomy.

They have also found the Mind Detox to be a great barometer for measuring how far they have drifted from their path. Clients have found that by using the Mind Detox when they start to feel life is becoming emotionally difficult, they are able to see where their minds have wandered off to and how this then drives how they feel emotionally. But one day of the Mind Detox and they feel back on track and good habits are re-started.

Use the step-by-step instructions below and the Detox Ingredients in the previous chapter to set up your day in the Detox Plan. The actual Plan is colour coded to help with this process. If you can, print out the Plan and keep it with you throughout the day. This makes it easier to refer to and keep you on track. And remember, as with any diet the more you put into it, the more you will get out. But the main objective is to enjoy yourself and the space this diet creates in your day.

The Day Before Preparations (Blue Sections)

1. Plan your meals for the day in the blue *Day Schedule* section. Use the

information from *Ingredient 6: Sleep, Diet and Exercise* to help you fill out this section. A little light food shopping is suggested; stock up on some fresh fruit and vegetables and think carefully about what you want to eat.

2. Fill in the blue Activities section using the information from *Ingredient 2: Meditation, Ingredient 3: Self Nourishment* and *Ingredient 4: Self Care.* Then fill these activities into the *Day Schedule* so you have a rough idea of when you are going to do them. These activities can always be changed during the day if you have a change of heart or find the choices you have made no longer feel right. Just return to the Detox Ingredients and re-pick.

3. We recommend that the night before you turn off all electronic devices (laptops, computers, and tablets) and pop them in a drawer out of sight. This reduces the desire to take a quick peek when you are walking past. You can keep your phones on you for making and receiving calls, setting alarms and using guided meditations. Try to resist using them for social media or internet browsing though!

4. We also suggest you think of your Intention the night before and write this on your plan in the blue *Intention for the Day* section so that when you wake up your intention is set and you are ready to go. You can find more about this in *Ingredient 1: Self Awareness* and there are suggested Intentions in the Detox Supplements section.

On the Day (Red Sections)

1. Start the day by filling out your affirmations in the red *Affirmations* section. For more information on this ingredient, go to *Ingredient 5: Affirmations and Gratitude* in the previous chapter. You can choose up to 4 affirmations and we have put together a list of all different kinds of affirmations in the Detox Supplements section to help you. But of course you can always make up your own!

2. The red *Check-In* section is explained in *Ingredient 1: Self-Awareness* and is filled in throughout the day as often as possible. Doing this check-in often can really have a significant impact. The more often you check in, the clearer it is to see how often your mind wanders from the task at

hand and the fluctuations in mood and transient nature of thought. It can be hard sometimes to describe how you are feeling though, so there is a comprehensive Emotions List in the Detox Supplements section to help you.

3. The *End of Day Check-Out* is best completed at the end of the day just before hopping into bed but can be done early the next day when your experience is still fresh in your mind. Write down any comments or learnings you want to remember from the day.

4. And last but by no means least, there's your gratitude list. This can be completed during the day but also as the last thing you do before bed, whichever feels right. Information on the benefits of gratitude can be found in *Ingredient 5: Affirmations and Gratitude*.

To Abide by Throughout the Day (Yellow Sections)

In the yellow sections you will find some useful rules to help you stick to your Mind Detox more easily. Abiding by these simple rules will help you stay focused on your goals and remain present.

Twin Tales

We've been doing the Mind Detox day as often as we can for quite some time now, and we've both been surprised at how hard it can be to do fully for a whole day. Although neither of us can lay claim to iron-cast willpower, we still didn't think it'd be quite so difficult to avoid a quick scroll through Facebook or collapse in front of the TV at the end of a long day.

As Charles Duhigg notes in *The Power of Habit*, the line between habit and addiction is much fainter than we think, and trying to change a seemingly innocuous habit can be as difficult as trying to combat an addiction to sugar.

Biological factors can also add to our difficulties. Recent research* (analysing over half a billion tweets on Twitter across the globe!) has confirmed exactly what we both found in trying to do the Mind Detox. Positive moods peak somewhere between 6am and 9am, and then gradually decline to a slump in the afternoon before rising again in the evening. We'd often start the Detox Day with a strong determination to follow our plan but by 3-4pm it's all but disappeared, and we'd slip into an unmotivated state and even sometimes forget that we were on the Mind Diet Detox!

It's really useful to have prepared defences against these mood changes, engrained habits and lapses in willpower. It might take a few attempts, but you'll quickly become aware of which parts of the Mind Detox you find difficult to stick to (and what time of the day your lapses occur). Make sure you take note of these, and have prepared defences such as alternative pick-me-ups to unhealthy afternoon snacking, or planning a sunset walk to reinvigorate you in the evening.

* *Diurnal and Seasonal Mood Vary with Work, Sleep and Daylength Across Diverse Cultures* - Scott A. Golder, Michael W. Macy

Mind Detox Plan

Day Schedule			Mindful Check-I	
	Time	Detail	Time	Doing?
Breakfast:				
Lunch:				
Dinner				

Activities

Meditation:

Self-Nourishment:

Self Care:

Exercise:

Affirmations

1. _____

_____

2. _____

_____

3. _____

_____

4. _____

_____

Intention for the Day

Blue - to fill in before day starts
Red - to fill in throughout the day
Yellow - to abide by all day

...inking?	Feeling?

Diet Baddies

No social media
No TV
No internet browsing
No computer (if possible)
No alcohol or drugs
No junk food

Diet Goodies

Be present & aware
Love & value yourself
Free yourself from caring about what other people think
Remain open to new experiences
Be generous of spirit
Spend time on relationships rather than distraction & consumerism

End of Day Check Out

Did you learn anything about yourself? What aspect of the detox diet did you find the most difficult? _____

_____

_____

_____

_____

Gratitude

What are you grateful for? (can be filled in at any time but make sure you have at least 3 things by the end of the day)

5. Detox Supplements

This section contains some useful support to help you on your Detox day, including an Affirmations List, an Emotions List, and an Intentions List.

Affirmations List

For Self-Love

I accept myself unconditionally right now
I am enough
I know in my heart that I am enough
I am healthy and filled with energy
I love myself deeply and unconditionally
I will offer myself love and compassion

For Happiness

I am in charge of my own happiness
I choose to be happy
I have the freedom and power to create the life I desire
I am calm and mindful
I wake up with a peaceful mind and a grateful heart

For Inspiration

My possibilities are endless
I am powerful, confident, and capable of reaching all my dreams
The future is good, I look forward with hope and happiness
I am moving closer to my dreams
I wake up today with intention and purpose
I am powerful in so many ways

For Self-Esteem

I am enough
I accept myself

I don't need anyone else's approval but my own
I am worthy of love
I am grateful for who I am and what I have
I am completely loveable just as I am today
I don't need others to validate my self-worth
I don't need to please everyone all of the time

For Achieving Your Goals and Self Belief
I am in the process of becoming the best version of myself
I am confident and courageous and have the ability to achieve my dreams
I can create a life I love
I am worthy of my dreams
I have the freedom and power to create the life I desire
I believe in myself and my ability to succeed
I am fearless
I let go of fearing mistakes and failure

For Anxiety and Depression
I am calm and mindful
I let go of all negativity that rests in my body and mind
I am safe
I breathe in calmness and breathe out worry
I am free of worry and at peace with who am I
I am flawed and make mistakes and that is ok
I acknowledge that the only constant in life is change and I accept this

For Getting Through Tough Times
This too shall pass
There are no blocks I cannot overcome
Challenges are the opportunities to grow and improve
I have the ability to overcome any challenges life presents to me
I can cope
I have the strength to overcome adversity

For Grief
I choose to heal my hurt spirit
I am grateful that you were in my life

I'll never be the same person again, and that's ok
I will always have the love I gained from having you in my life
I'm surrounded by support and love that will help me to heal
I will be gentle with myself as I heal

Compassion for others
I love my partner exactly as s/he is and enjoy his/her unique qualities
We are all one
May I try and be non-judgmental
I will listen with an open heart
May I show kindness to others
The difficulty in others is not a personal reflection of me

Others
May I be happy, may I be healthy, may I be safe
I am my awareness
My thoughts do not define me
I have nothing to prove and nothing to hide
I am grounded and centred
I will continue to change and grow from a place of acceptance

Emotions List

Positive	Negative		Not Quite One or the Other
Accepted	Aggressive	Inadequate	Bored
Amazed	Alienated	Inferior	Confused
Comfortable	Angry	Insecure	Distant
Confident	Annoyed	Irritated	Lethargic
Content	Anxious	Jealous	Embarrassed
Daring	Apathetic	Lonely	Nervous
Delighted	Ashamed	Miserable	Relieved
Eager	Bereft	Overwhelmed	Startled
Ecstatic	Bitter	Petrified	Surprised
Elated	Alarmed	Powerless	Determined
Energetic	Cross	Regret	Hungry
Excited	Depressed	Rejected	Restless
Glad	Despairing	Remorseful	Thirsty
Happy	Disappointed	Resentful	Wistful
Hopeful	Discontent	Sad	
Inspired	Disdainful	Scared	
Joyful	Disgusted	Self-conscious	
Loving	Disillusioned	Shocked	
Motivated	Envious	Stressed	
Optimistic	Fearful	Stupid	
Overjoyed	Flat	Suspicious	
Peaceful	Foolish	Tearful	
Playful	Frazzled	Tense	
Proud	Frustrated	Terrified	
Respected	Furious	Threatened	
Safe	Grieving	Tired	
Satisfied	Guilty	Trapped	
Secure	Harassed	Uncomfortable	
Silly	Horrified	Vulnerable	
Strong	Humiliated	Weepy	
Wonderful	Hurt	Worried	
	Ignored	Worthless	

Intentions List

Our intention creates our reality.
Wayne Dyer

This section will help you with setting an intention for your Detox Day, part of the Self-Awareness Ingredient. We've laid out a list of possibilities, but please remember these are just ideas, and if none take your fancy then please create your own.

What is an Intention?

Think of an intention as the fuel to manifesting your goals and visions or as a guiding principle for your day. Setting an intention is like selecting the destination before you set off, it gives you the direction you wish to go in and something to return to if you feel you are traveling off course. As this intention is just for your Mind Diet Detox Day, we've set out some examples below to inspire you focused on short-term intentions, rather than longer-term intentions (but if you wish to do a long-term intention and continue it on after the Detox Day please do!).

Happiness & Awareness

I intend to remain conscious and aware today.
I intend to be present for as much of the day as I can.
I intend to remain mindful today.
Today I will accept whatever happens as if I had chosen it.
I will try to remain positive and not allow negative thoughts to cloud my mind today.
I intend not to take anything personally today.
Today, I will not stress over things I cannot control.
I intend to be grateful for the small things today.
I intend to be grateful for all the positive (and negative!) things in my life today.
I will recognise any labels or judgements I make today, and release them.
I intend to learn from any challenges today.

Relationships

I intend to listen with my full attention to everyone I interact with today.
I will truly listen when someone is talking to me instead of thinking of what I want to say next.
I intend to be kind to myself and others today.
I intend to show acts of kindness today, bringing joy into the life of another whenever I can.
I intend to use kindness in all my interactions.
I intend to be as honest and open as I can in all my interactions today.
My intention is to show unconditional love to my partner, family and friends today.
I intend to fully enjoy my relationship with my partner today.
I intend to remain patient with my children today.

Work & Health

I intend to lead by example today.
I intend to be open to success and abundance today.
I intend to believe in myself and my ability to fulfil my dreams today.
I intend to be thankful for my work today, whatever it is.

6. Mind Diet Pantry

In this section we wanted to share with you some of the books, people and other tools we have used over the years that have helped us on our journeys of self-discovery. We know how daunting it can be to walk into a bookstore or go online looking for something that will be 'helpful' but have no idea where to start so we thought we would give you our list of experts and other useful tools.

This is by no means exhaustive but just some of the amazing resources we have found that have helped us on our journey!

People

Ajahn Brahm
Ajahn Brahm is a British/Australian Theravada Buddhist monk based at Bodhinyana Monastery just outside Perth in Western Australia. They do great retreat weekends there and, if you are lucky, you will get to hear Ajahn Brahm talk. His talks are witty and insightful and accessible to beginners and more advanced thinkers.

Alain de Botton
Alain de Botton is a Swiss-born British philosopher and author who writes about modern day experiences using a philosophical edge. His work on love and relationships in a modern world are fascinating investigations into what our expectations are and how far from reality we have drifted. His School of Life, described as a 'toolkit for life' provides lessons on topics such as work and relationships, with the aim of helping develop emotional intelligence.

Alan Watts

Alan Watts was a British philosopher who was one of the first people to bring Eastern Philosophy to a Western audience, particularly the ancient Hindu philosophy of Vedanta. An independent thinker, his books, including 'The Way of Zen', and 'The Book on the Taboo against knowing who you are' offer deeply, mind-opening ways of thinking about the world and our place in it.

Arianna Huffington

Arianna Huffington is a Greek-American author and business woman. She co-founded The Huffington Post but after two years of running it she collapsed at her desk, hitting her head and breaking a cheekbone. She had suffered burnout and soon became an advocate for the benefits of sleep and wellness, setting up Thrive Global, an organisation designed to help corporations and individuals enhance wellbeing and performance. Her own personal experience of ignoring her body's signs of exhaustion have given her first-hand experience of something she is now able to impart to others.

Brene Brown

Brene Brown is an American research professor at the University of Houston. She first came to our attention, along with over 30 million other people, with her TED talk on vulnerability. This talk is funny and insightful and shows us the importance of vulnerability and the positive impact is has on our ability to connect with others authentically. She has also researched other topics such as courage, shame and empathy and is a New York Times bestseller.

Dalai Lama

The Dalai Lama is the spiritual leader of Tibet who describes himself as 'a simple Buddhist monk'. The Dalai Lama has spoken extensively around the world about the teachings of Buddha and garners respect from all areas for his gentle nature and compassion for all beings. His talks are enlightening with his trademark sense of humour always present.

Dan Harris

Dan Harris is an American TV anchor who in 2004 had a panic attack live on air. His journey from this point into the whys and hows led him on a path he never expected. We like him because his take on 'self-help' is from a sceptic's point of view. He has never been a fan of what he perceived to be 'ridiculous crystal healing, dream catchers' but meditation has changed his life and he now speaks about all the reasons why someone would not want to go down this path but should. He is able to reach an audience that others cannot simply because he was that audience.

Dan Siegel

Dan Siegel is an American clinical professor of psychiatry at the UCLA School of Medicine and Executive Director of the Mindsight Institute. We first found him on the Mindfulness Summit and his Wheel of Awareness meditation has proved to be invaluable on our journey of growth. The Wheel of Awareness explores our relationship to all that is known to us from an awareness perspective using the metaphor of a wheel with the hub being our experience of awareness and the spokes being all that we can be aware of.

Deepak Chopra

Deepak Chopra is an Indian-born American and one of the best-known figures in the alternative health and wellbeing industry. Starting off as a doctor in traditional medicine, he moved quickly into more alternative health spheres such as meditation, and has since become one of the most prominent authors and speakers in the field. He has published many books mainly focused on mind-body healing and alternative health, and speaks all over the world.

Eckhart Tolle

Eckhart Tolle is a German born spiritual teacher. After years of depression and mental health problems at the age of 29 Eckhart had a profound inner transformation. He spent the next few years gaining understanding of this new way of being and has become one of the most influential spiritual teachers of modern time. We first saw him talk back in the late 90s. Our mother had booked tickets for us and we showed up not knowing a thing about him. But we do remember being mesmerised by every word he said. Such an unassuming man with a gentle voice that managed to fill an auditorium and keep 1200 people rapt for 2 hours.

Jack Kornfield
Jack Kornfield is an American-born Buddhist practitioner who trained as a monk in the monasteries of Thailand, India and Burma. He talks about being at University and recognising that a huge part of his education was not being acknowledged and this led him to Buddhism and his own journey of self-discovery. Jack has one of those voices we could listen to for hours! His talks on compassion and inner-kindness are fantastic for those moments when your inner critic gets too noisy.

Jon Kabat-Zinn
Jon Kabat-Zinn is an American professor emeritus of medicine and the creator of the Stress Reduction Clinic and Centre for Mindfulness in Medicine, Health Care and Society at the University of Massachusetts Medical School. He has been largely responsible got bringing mindfulness to the western world and again, like with everyone on this list, you can find some really interesting talks online that he has done at various Universities all over the world.

Joseph Goldstein
Joseph Goldstein is an American Vipassana teacher and co-founder of the Insight Meditation Society with Jack Kornfield and Sharon Salzberg. We first found Joseph on the Mindfulness Summit too where he spoke beautifully about the importance of loving kindness. Along with so many of the meditation and mindfulness teachers his gentle approach leaves you feeling safe and nourished.

Kristin Neff
Kristin Neff is an American born associate professor in the Educational Psychology Department at University of Texas who specialises in self-compassion. Her talks on self-compassion have really helped us deepen our understanding and her website has some really useful free resources if you are interested in furthering your understanding.

Prof Mark Williams
Mark Williams is an English professor of Clinical Psychology and Welcome Trust Principal Research Fellow at Oxford University. He is also the co-developer of MBCT (Mindfulness Based Cognitive Therapy)

and his book 'Mindfulness, Finding Peace in a Frantic World' with Danny Penman was one of the first books we read around mindfulness. We found it easy to read and gave great examples of negative thought patterns and how to recognise them that really resonated with us.

Melli O'Brien

Melli O'Brien is an Australian meditation and yoga teacher and co-founder of the Mindfulness Summit, an online resource that gives thousands of people access to mindfulness. We have both accessed this summit over the years and found the talks extremely helpful and inspirational and try and return as often as possible. She also has her own website mrsmindfulness.com where she offers information and retreats to help deepen your practice.

Oprah Winfrey

Oprah Winfrey is an American all-round superstar, she is a media proprietor, talk show host, actress, producer and philanthropist but what brought her to our attention for this book was her Super Soul Sunday interviews. These interviews are designed to explore issues including spirituality, the afterlife and personal fulfilment and she has interviewed several people on this list. Through these interviews we see her own journey into self and her questions to the experts she speaks to show she is as in-tune as they are.

Pema Chodron

Pema Chodron is an American Tibetan monk who has written several books and also speaks extensively around the world. She has a gentle authority on topics ranging from 'dealing with difficult emotions' to 'becoming limitless'.

Dr. Rick Hanson

Rick Hanson is an American psychologist, author and senior fellow/ meditation teacher at the Greater Good Science Centre at UC Berkeley. His work around resilience and hardwiring happiness has made him a New York Times bestseller. We first found him on TEDx doing his talk on Hardwiring Happiness where he speaks about his own experience as a child of feeling 'left out' and how he changed his feelings from mainly negative to mainly positive.

Dr. Ron Siegel
Ron Siegel is an American assistant professor of Psychology part time at Harvard University. He is also a long-time student of mindfulness and meditation and sits on the board of directors and faculty of the Institute for Meditation and Psychotherapy. His easy manner makes him approachable and easy to listen to. His talks online, especially the science behind mindfulness, are informative and give a great all-round understanding of what mindfulness is and how it works.

Ruby Wax
Ruby Wax is an American-born actress, comedian, producer and writer who has lived in the UK for over 40 years. In more recent years she has gone back to school and studied to get her masters in Mindfulness Based Cognitive Therapy from Oxford University where she met Mark Williams, who is also on our list. We have seen her talk at various festivals around the UK and her natural stage presence and humour give her talks an easy going and accessible edge to some usually difficult topics such as depression and anxiety. She is fast becoming an important voice in the global mindfulness movement.

Shawn Achor
Shawn Achor is an American happiness researcher, author and speaker who co-founded the Institute for Applied Positive Research which sounds like a really fun job. We first heard his talk on TEDxBloomington where he spoke about what happiness is and how it is measured and therefore applied. His upbeat attitude and cheerful persona make what he says about happiness more profound and you immediately want to start applying his tools to your own life. In essence you can see he practices what he preaches.

Tara Brach
Tara Brach is an American Psychologist who blends Western psychology and Eastern spiritual practices. She works closely with Jack Kornfield and runs courses on mindfulness meditation which you can access online. Mindfulness Daily was a course Fran did and still uses often with herself and clients whenever she felt her practice slipping.

Thich Nhat Hanh

Thich Nhat Hanh is a Vietnamese Buddhist monk and peace activist. He is one of the world's most influencial spiritual leaders with a focus on peace and compassion. His own story started at the age of 7 when he felt the calling to become a monk and the civil war in Vietnam in the early 60's drove him to lead one of the great non-violent resistance movements of the 20th century. He has written over 100 books, any of which would be an asset to your library.

Websites

Online there are also a plethora of useful sites and free courses but these are ones we have specifically used over the years and go back to again and again:

https://themindfulnesssummit.com/
The mindfulness summit now has over 500,000 followers. It's a fantastic free resource that offers incredible summits and access to some of the greatest speakers and practitioners in the field.

http://franticworld.com/
The FranticWorld website is developed from the work of Mark Williams, Danny Penman and Vidyamala Burch and explains mindfulness and the benefits of meditation. It also offers free meditations and explains why and how these can help.

http://www.drdansiegel.com/resources/wheel_of_awareness/
The wheel of awareness came up via a talk we saw Dan do and when we tried it we found it really helpful in describing the various ways we can harness our awareness. Again, this is free when you sign up and is a really great edition to your meditation practice.

http://www.freemindfulness.org/home
This is a wonderful website full of free meditations from various sources all over the world.

http://www.fragrantheart.com/cms/free-audio-meditations
This is another lovely site with a selection of free meditations varying

from a 1 minute calming meditation to sending love to your favourite wild animal.

https://self-compassion.org
This is the website of Kristin Neff where you will find some really useful resources on how to understand and develop self-compassion as well as lots of other great information and upcoming talks and workshops.

Apps & Podcasts

There are also some great meditation apps and podcasts for the phone:

Apps	*Podcasts*
Buddhify	Oprah's Super Soul Conversations
Breethe	10% Happier with Dan Harris
Calm	Live Happy Now
Headspace	
Insight timer	
MindBell	
Mindbliss	
Oak	

Books

These are just some of the books (out of the many wonderful ones available) that we recommend.

The Art of Meditation – The Art of Happiness - Matthieu Ricard

Emotional Intelligence – Daniel Goleman

Full Catastrophe Living - Jon Kabat-Zinn

The Gifts of Imperfection - Brene Brown

The Happiness Advantage - Shawn Achor

Hardwiring Happiness - Rick Hanson

Leave Your Mind Behind - Matthew McKay PhD and Catharine Sutker

The Life Changing Magic of Tidying - Maria Kondo

Mindfulness. A Practical Guide to Finding Peace in a Frantic World - Mark Williams and Danny Penman

A Mindfulness Guide for the Frazzled - Ruby Wax

Modern Mindfulness - Rohan Gunatillake

Practising the Power of Now - Eckhart Tolle

Resilient - Rick Hanson

The Science of Mindfulness and Self-Compassion: How to Build New Habits to Transform Your Life – Kristin Neff and Shauna Shapiro

Super Brain: Unleash the Explosive Power of Your Mind – Deepak Chopra & Rudolph E. Tanzi

The Things You Can See Only When You Slow Down - Haemin Sunim

The Ultimate Happiness Prescription - Deepak Chopra

What is Mindfulness? – Dr. Tamara Russell

The Wisdom of Sundays - Oprah Winfrey

Why We Sleep: The New Science of Sleep and Dreams - Matthew Walker

Printed in Poland
by Amazon Fulfillment
Poland Sp. z o.o., Wrocław